PROFILES

Helen Keller

Carolyn Sloan

Illustrated by
Karen Heywood

Hamish Hamilton
London

Titles in the Profiles *series*

Edith Cavell	0-241-11479-9	Montgomery of Alamein	0-241-11562-0
Marie Curie	0-241-11741-0	The Queen Mother	0-241-11030-0
Roald Dahl	0-241-11043-2	Florence Nightingale	0-241-11477-2
Thomas Edison	0-241-10713-X	Emmeline Pankhurst	0-241-11478-0
Anne Frank	0-241-11294-X	Pope John Paul II	0-241-10711-3
Elizabeth Fry	0-241-12084-5	Anna Pavlova	0-241-10481-5
Indira Gandhi	0-241-11772-0	Prince Philip	0-241-11167-6
Gandhi	0-241-11166-8	Beatrix Potter	0-241-12051-9
Basil Hume	0-241-11204-4	Lucinda Prior-Palmer	0-241-10710-5
Amy Johnson	0-241-12317-8	Viv Richards	0-241-12046-2
Helen Keller	0-241-11295-8	Barry Sheene	0-241-10851-9
John Lennon	0-241-11561-2	Mother Teresa	0-241-10933-7
Martin Luther King	0-241-10931-0	Queen Victoria	0-241-10480-7
Nelson Mandela	0-241-11913-8	The Princess of Wales	0-241-11740-2
Bob Marley	0-241-11476-4		

HAMISH HAMILTON CHILDREN'S BOOKS

Penguin Books Ltd, 27 Wrights Lane, London W8 5TZ (Publishing & Editorial)
and Harmondsworth, Middlesex, England (Distribution & Warehouse)
Viking Penguin Inc., 40 West 23rd Street, New York, New York 10010, U.S.A.
Penguin Books Australia Ltd, Ringwood, Victoria, Australia
Penguin Books Canada Limited, 2801 John Street, Markham, Ontario, Canada L3R 1B4
Penguin Books (N.Z.) Ltd, 182—190 Wairau Road, Auckland 10, New Zealand

First published in Great Britain 1984 by
Hamish Hamilton Children's Books

Copyright © 1984 text by Carolyn Sloan
Copyright © 1984 illustrations by Karen Heywood

Reprinted 1986, 1987

British Library Cataloguing in Publication Data

Sloan, Carolyn
Helen Keller. — (Profiles)
2. Blind-deaf — United States — Biography
— Juvenile literature
I. Title   II. Series
362.4'092'4   HV1624.K4

ISBN 0-241-11295-8

Typeset by Pioneer
Printed in Great Britain at the
University Press, Cambridge

Contents

1 Helen

Helen Keller was born in the little one-street town of Tuscumbia, in the southern American state of Alabama. It was 1880, fifteen years after the Civil War in which her father had fought as a Captain in the Confederate army. Helen's mother, his second wife, was twenty years younger, a lively, intelligent woman who worked hard running the house and raising everything the family needed on their small farm.

Helen was a bright and inquisitive baby. At six months she could say 'how d'ye', 'tea' and 'wah-wah' which meant water. On her first birthday she took her first steps, tottering after the dancing shadows of leaves on the floor. But her carefree childhood was not to last. Helen had just one spring to hear the mocking bird's song, one summer to see the fruit and flowers, and one autumn to watch the changing leaves. And then on a February day, when she was nineteen months old, she caught a mysterious fever that raged so fiercely the doctor thought she might die. But the fever went as suddenly as it had come. The Kellers' relief was short-lived. A few days later they realised that the illness had left Helen completely deaf and blind.

Later in her life Helen vaguely remembered it

happening. It was like a dream, it was always night and she wondered why the day never came. Gradually she got used to the darkness and silence. Her baby talk ceased when she could no longer hear it. The only sounds she made were instinctive ones — laughter, crying, screaming. She was too young to realise that tragedy had struck her alone. Other people went on seeing, hearing, talking. But she was shut away from them in a dark, silent, lonely world of her own. She could still smell and touch things though, and as she grew she used these senses to discover the world about her.

She followed her mother around all day, clutching on to her long skirts. She touched and smelled everything she came across, and felt other people's hands to find out what they were doing. With her mother's loving patience, and help from the cook's little girl, Martha, she learned how to milk the cows and feed the chickens. She could knead the dough in the kitchen, and she learned to sort out her own clothes from the laundry, fold them and put them away. She loved playing with dolls, but guarded them jealously, and when she found her new baby sister asleep in her cradle, she tipped her on to the floor in a fury.

Helen could be naughty: the day she discovered how keys worked, she locked her mother in the larder and sat on the steps chuckling as she felt the vibrations of Mrs Keller pounding on the door. Another day when she was cutting out paper dolls, she suddenly turned to her friend Martha and cut off all her corkscrew curls. In spite of her handicaps, Helen was clever. Her quick,

10

Helen's mother

curious fingers explored everything, especially people.
She liked to feel their clothes, their faces and hair, and
she would remember them. She invented her own sign
language with over sixty signs which the family could

Helen as a little girl

understand. Pulling her hair into a knot meant her mother. Pretending to put on a pair of glasses meant her father. She would describe 'small' by pinching a little bit of skin on the back of her hand.

Helen could be sweet and loving — and she could be a raging beast. An uncle said she was mentally defective and should be put away, because it was 'not nice to see'. But an understanding aunt insisted that she had more sense than any of the Kellers, if only there was a way to reach her mind. Helen's early childhood must have been desperately lonely and boring, yet she had the courage and intelligence to make the best of it. But when she was five she realised that she was different from other people, and it made her angry and even violent. She would sit between two people who were talking to each other and put her hands on their faces. She felt their lips moving, their expressions changing, and she knew that they had a way of communicating with each other. She wanted to do it too, but no matter how she moved her lips, she could hear no sound, see no reaction. She would work herself into a frenzy of frustration, hurling herself about kicking and screaming, until she broke down in tears of misery and frustration. She was becoming impossible to control, and her parents could only watch helplessly and give in to her tantrums.

They took her to a famous eye specialist, but he said he could do nothing for her sight. It had gone for ever. He urged them to go and see Dr Alexander Graham Bell, the man who invented the telephone. Both his mother and his wife were deaf, and he was concerned with teaching the deaf. Helen and Dr Bell became instant friends. 'He understood my signs' she wrote later, 'and I knew it and loved him at once.'

Dr Bell contacted the Director of the Perkins Institute for the Blind in Boston, Mr Anagnos. A deaf and blind girl, Laura Bridgman, had been educated at the Institute and still lived there. Her brilliant teacher had died, but Dr Bell asked whether another very special teacher might be found to teach little Helen Keller. Mr Anagnos thought he knew just the right person — Annie Sullivan.

2 Annie

The Sullivan family had fled from famine in Ireland to seek a better life in America. But when Anne Mansfield was born in 1866 they were living in squalid poverty. The next two children died, the third was healthy and then Jimmy was born; he had a tubercular hip and was crippled like his mother. Annie's father was unskilled, a drinker and violent brawler. The family was haunted by tragedy. When Annie was five she got the eye disease trachoma. Her mother could only treat it with geranium water and by the time she was eight she was half blind — and half wild with temper tantrums. Then her mother died and poverty finally split the family up. Annie and Jimmy were sent to Tewksbury Almshouse — 'the poorhouse'.

Annie fought viciously when she learned she was to be separated from Jimmy, and he was allowed a cot next to hers in the women's ward. Tewksbury was badly overcrowded with people who were dying, diseased or mad. The only place for Annie and Jimmy to play was 'The Dead House' where corpses were prepared for burial. But Annie was used to poverty, many of the women were Irish and Catholic like herself, and she had Jimmy to care for.

But then Jimmy died. His cot was simply trundled away in the night; there was no priest to bury him or to console Annie, who felt so completely alone that she wanted to die too. A year later she had several operations on her eyes. But they were unsuccessful. For the next five years she was officially listed as blind and lived at Tewksbury where, amongst the horrors, she discovered a library — and a girl who was only half mad to read to her. Annie learned there were schools for the blind where she could learn to read too, and when some Inspectors toured the Almshouse she hurled herself at them demanding to go to school. For once, Annie was lucky. They listened to her and found her a place at the Perkins Institute for the Blind in Boston. Annie left, wearing coarse clothes provided by a charity and with advice ringing in her ears . . . 'Keep your head up, you're as good as anyone. Don't tell anyone you came from the poorhouse!'

Perkins was famous for its first Director, Dr Howe, who had been a pioneer in educating neglected blind children and giving them skills to earn a living. He had also taken on the seemingly impossible task of educating Laura Bridgman who was deaf, blind and had little sense of smell or taste. He gave her a spoon and a key with S-P-O-O-N and K-E-Y written in raised letters and stuck to them. He made her stroke the letters over and over, until she realised that they were different. Then he gave her the same words in raised print on pieces of card, and she learned to match the words to the things. After many months of patient work, Dr Howe showed Laura that everything had a

Annie Sullivan

name, and a name was a word that made up language which she could use to express herself. Once Laura had mastered this, her sombre face became lively — at the age of eight, she was beginning to live. Now Dr Howe could teach her the 'manual language' which had been invented by some Spanish monks who had taken a vow of silence. He spelled words into the palm of her hand, and she learnt to spell them back into his hand so they could have a 'conversation'.

Dr Howe had died before Annie went to Perkins and his son-in-law Mr Anagnos was the new director. It was hard for Annie to adapt to the new life. At fourteen she was more ignorant than the youngest child. She had never worn a nightdress, used a needle, owned a comb. She was not used to being told to do things and often rebelled; she was so rude that Anagnos called her Miss Spitfire. Her behaviour was often so bad that she should have been asked to leave, but Anagnos realised that once tamed, Annie could be one of their most talented pupils. She always got another chance. For two years she did her lessons in braille, but after two operations on her eyes, she was able to read with them instead of her fingers. She became friendly with Laura Bridgman and learnt the manual language so that she could spell the school gossip into her hand. Laura was fifty then, a frail person who made extremely fine lace, but had never become independent enough to leave the Institution.

When Annie was twenty she graduated from Perkins and made a farewell speech that stunned the audience with the richness of its language. When Anagnos was asked if he could find a teacher for Helen Keller, he at once thought of his 'Miss Spitfire'. Annie was not sure if she could take on such a challenge but she was willing, and returned to Perkins to study Dr Howe's detailed reports about Laura Bridgman's education. In March 1887 she was ready to leave for the unknown South, and her special pupil.

3 Helen and Annie

There was such excitement in the Keller household that Helen knew someone special was expected. She stood on the porch all day waiting for the vibrations of approaching footsteps. Annie was excited too and rushed to hug her, but she was pushed away as Helen reached to feel her face, her hair, her clothes and rummage in her bag. She followed Annie upstairs, helped her to unpack and tried on her hat. Annie soon learnt Helen's 'signs' so that they could make each other understand simple things, and Annie was thrilled to find how bright and responsive Helen was.

But she had not seen the other Helen, who did exactly as she wanted and threw tantrums if she was checked. Yet Annie was ready for the first scene. She had made up her mind that Helen must learn to obey her right from the beginning. It would be impossible to try and teach a child she could not control.

At breakfast, Helen ate with her fingers and grabbed food from other people's plates. When Annie stopped her, she kicked and screamed, bit and punched. Annie slapped her soundly, the dining-room became a battlefield and the distraught parents fled. Annie eventually won, but they both ended up in tears. The same scenes started whenever Annie wanted Helen to comb her hair, or button her boots. Helen screamed and fought. Annie insisted firmly. Mrs Keller wept. Captain Keller interfered. Annie's task seemed doomed to failure — to everyone except Annie. She had found a little garden house in the grounds and announced that she and Helen would go and live there alone. It was the only way Annie could hope to make progress. Helen was taken a roundabout way to the house. The furniture was moved about so that she didn't know where she was — or that her anxious parents often came to watch her through the windows.

In two weeks, Annie and Helen were becoming the friends they would be for life. Helen could still be wild and naughty, but with Annie, she realised, it was more

The garden house

fun to be good. They spent most of their time outdoors, walking in the woods, or romping in the grass. Annie was always showing her things — flowers, puddles, insects that buzzed in her hand. She taught Helen to sew and crochet, and they did gymnastics each morning. And all the time Annie spelled words into Helen's hand.

It was a game to Helen. She spelled them back to Annie, but she did not know that they meant anything. One day, a month after Annie had arrived, she was

The water pump

patiently trying to explain to Helen that the word M-U-G meant the mug, and that W-A-T-E-R was the wet stuff inside it. But still Helen couldn't see the difference. They went for a walk near the well house where somebody was pumping water. Annie took Helen's hand and held it under the spout. She took her other hand and spelled W-A-T-E-R into it, slowly at first and then faster and faster. A miracle happened. Helen's face lit up with excitement and delight. The mystery of language was suddenly solved. She knew that the water flowing over her hand had a name, W-A-T-E-R.

Helen rushed about touching things and asking Annie what they were called. A whole new life had suddenly opened up for her. A few weeks later Annie reported to Anagnos that 'the wild little creature has been transformed into a gentle child. The manual alphabet is a key to everything she wants to know. She is a truly wonderful child.' By then Helen knew about 300 words and was learning new ones at the rate of five a day. When Annie spelled into her hand, she used complete sentences even though she knew that Helen could only understand a few words. She had decided to teach Helen language in the same way a mother teaches a baby. The mother talks endlessly to the baby, using words he doesn't understand. Gradually he learns a few, and then learns to put them together until he uses proper sentences.

It was not long before Helen learnt to read raised type, and Annie gave her cards with different words so she could try and make sentences. It was still a game —

but Annie realised how well Helen was progressing when she found her standing in a wardrobe one day. She had pinned two cards saying THE and GIRL to her dress, and arranged the cards saying IS IN THE WARDROBE on the shelf.

Helen's fascination with words made her into a 'chatterbox'. She started spelling the moment she got up, and if Annie could not reply she would answer her own questions and have a conversation with herself.

Annie reported on Helen's progress regularly to Anagnos, and he sent her teaching equipment from Perkins. The rate at which Helen was learning impressed the staff at Perkins. They couldn't hear enough about her enthusiasm and personality, and they became more and more excited as they realised that Helen Keller was going to be an even greater success story than Laura Bridgman.

4 Helen's New World

The summer of 1887 was all adventure for Helen. Annie did not believe in classroom lessons; she taught Helen all the time by doing things with her, and describing every detail into her hand. Helen had always had a special feeling for all kinds of wildlife. Animals had been her companions in her isolated years. Now Annie could tell her how the birds lived and made their nests, and how the sun and rain made seeds grow. One of their favourite walks was to Keller's Landing, a wharf on the river that had been used to land soldiers during the civil war. Here they had geography lessons. Annie made raised maps in the mud so that Helen could learn about mountains, oceans and rivers. She learned that there were other countries where people lived very different lives, and had different animals.

In November they went to a circus. The performers had heard about Helen and were determined she should enjoy it. She fed the elephants and rode one around the ring. The clowns and acrobats let her feel their costumes and she was thrilled with the monkeys because she could put her hands on them and feel them doing their tricks.

It was easy for Helen to learn words for objects, or

for things she could do like running or scratching. But when it came to words that couldn't be touched or done, Annie had to wait for an opportunity to introduce them. One day, Helen was stringing beads in such a complicated sequence that she frowned with concentration. Annie touched her forehead and wrote THINK firmly into her hand. She knew at once that this word described what was going on in her head — there were words for everything!

One day Annie gave Helen her own braille slate, thinking she would have fun pricking the braille symbols onto a piece of paper. Helen knew that Annie used it to write letters to the blind girls at Perkins and when she had filled a piece of paper full of holes she folded it and insisted on taking it to the post. Annie decided it was time she learned to write. She used a piece of paper fitted over a grooved writing board, and guided the pencil in the grooves with the forefinger of her left hand. The writing was called 'Square-hand' and Helen wrote her first letter to her mother when she was on a holiday. . .

Helen will write mother letter papa did give helen medicine mildred will sit in swing mildred will kiss helen teacher did give helen peach george is sick in bed . . . good-by

It was written just four months after Annie had come to teach her.

Helen's first Christmas with Annie was a joy for everyone. It was the first time she even knew what it was. She learned to dance and went to parties where

24

Captain Keller

other children had learned the manual language so that they could talk to her. The Kellers were moved to tears on Christmas morning. Captain Keller could not speak, he just grasped Annie's hand. Mrs Keller said, 'Miss Annie I thank God every day of my life for sending you to us. But I never realised until this morning what a blessing you have been to us.'

Annie often felt unsettled in Tuscumbia. She was a Yankee girl living in the South and often got into arguments about the civil war. She thought the Southerners were arrogant and talked down to women — and she hated the way they treated negroes as if they were still slaves. Helen knew that her family were white and their servants black. Questioned by Annie once about a visitor she thought perhaps he was blue! Later in life she was to fight for negro rights — and infuriate her Southern family.

Annie was also unsettled because of Helen. She wrote regularly to Anagnos reporting her progress and everyone at Perkins longed to meet this brilliant child. Annie wanted professional advice now with Helen's education, and special equipment for her to use. She had started reading and writing in braille and it was difficult to get the huge volumes sent to Tuscumbia. Helen was keen to go too. Urged perhaps by Annie she had started writing to the blind children.

Helen will write little blind girls a letter and teacher will come to see little blind girls helen and teacher will go in steam car to Boston helen and blind girls will have fun blind girls can talk on fingers. . . .

5 Helen and *The Frost King*

Helen and 'Teacher', as Annie was now called, arrived in Boston in 1888 to stay with Mr Anagnos. Helen was never officially a pupil at the Perkins Institute, but she spent a lot of time there over the next few years. She thought it was like arriving in her own country where the people spoke her language. She made friends with the blind children at once, and although they were not deaf, they understood her.

Helen loved travelling, there was so much to feel and smell, and Annie was always at her side with vivid descriptions of everything she saw. They had history outings from Boston to the battleground at Bunkers Hill, and went by steamboat to Plymouth Rock where the English Pilgrim Fathers had landed in 1620. Annie had tried to describe the sea to Helen, but when they went for a holiday at Cape Cod Helen got a shock when the waves seemed to seize her and toss her about. But she soon got over her fear because it was so exciting to feel the waves and the spray, the throb of the beach, and the pebbles rattling together. When she was older she would often go swimming alone, on the end of a rope. She was still bathing in the sea when she was over eighty.

Although Helen was completely deaf she liked 'listening' with her fingers to a cat purring or a dog barking. She would put her hands on a piano and beat time to the music that was being played. When she was ten she heard that a deaf and blind girl in Sweden had learnt to speak. Helen was determined to speak, too, and a special teacher, Miss Fuller, was found for her. The only way Miss Fuller could show Helen how sounds were formed was to put Helen's fingers inside her mouth to feel how she moved her tongue and her lips for each sound. In one lesson Helen learned six elements of speech, M, P, A, S, T, I.

But that was just the beginning. It took eleven more lessons before she stammered her first sentence, 'It is warm'. She practised for hours each day, talking to her toys, to trees, and even to stones, but it was months before even Annie and Miss Fuller could understand her — and years before she could speak confidently.

Helen had a naturally sweet and compassionate nature. When she went riding she would not allow a whip to be used on her pony. If another child had less presents than she did at a party, she would insist he or she had her own favourite one. When she heard that a little deaf and blind boy called Tommy was to be sent to an almshouse, she was heartbroken. There was no one to care for him, and no money to pay for him to have special education.

But it just so happened that Helen's dog, Lioness, had been shot by a policeman because it had been wandering in a town without a lead. Helen was very upset, but she wrote to the man who had given her

Lioness, saying she forgave the policeman who couldn't have known what a dear, good dog Lioness was. The letter was published and suddenly Helen and Lioness were news all over America, Canada and even in England. Money came pouring in to buy her another dog. Helen wrote and thanked the people who sent it, and told them how much she wanted to raise money for Tommy, whose need was so great. They responded and a fund was set up in Helen's name. Tommy was saved from the almshouse, and Helen, at the age of ten, had already started her mission in life to help the poor and handicapped, and persuade those who had everything to give to those who had nothing.

The following year, Helen's trusting world fell apart — all because of a fairy story. When Annie told her about the lovely colours of autumn leaves, she wrote a story about them. King Frost was sending jewels to Santa Claus to buy food for the poor to see them

Helen and her dog, Lioness

through the winter. But the fairies carrying the jewels stopped to play, and Mr Sun melted the jewels whose colours flowed into the autumn leaves. King Frost thought they were so beautiful that he came every year after that to paint the trees and comfort the world for the flight of summer.

Annie and the Kellers were so proud of Helen that they sent her story to Mr Anagnos as a birthday present. He had it published, and Helen, already a celebrity, became a sensation. A week later the magic of King Frost turned to black despair. A story almost exactly the same as Helen's had been printed in a book some years earlier. Helen was called a liar and a cheat. Annie was called a fraud who had taught her pupil to deceive. They were both questioned over and again at Perkins. There was a full Court of Enquiry, and Annie was taken away so that Helen could be questioned alone. It was a terrible ordeal for them both, even though it was finally discovered that Annie had never read the story. It had been read to Helen, though, by someone else, and Helen had stored the details away in her amazing memory. When Annie told her about the autumn colours, the story had come back to her, and she had written it down, believing it to be her own.

Suspicions lingered. Mr Anagnos had called Helen 'a living lie' and had accused Annie of making her one. It was the end of their friendship. Helen had been sheltered until then; she had not known there was dishonesty and cheating in the world, and to be accused of it herself was almost more than she could bear. She wept all night after the Enquiry, and hoped to die before morning.

6 From School to University

The Frost King scandal made Helen nervous about writing anything else. Annie encouraged her to write about her life for a magazine, *Youth's Companion*. That, at least, would be entirely her own, and Annie hoped it would give her confidence. Meanwhile they were cheered up by a visit to Dr Bell, and he and Helen arranged a surprise trip to Niagara Falls for Annie.

Annie painted a powerful word-picture of the grandeur and beauty of the Falls, and Helen could feel the power of the moving water that made the air tremble. She wrote a poem about Niagara for Dr Bell. He loved it, and quoted from it in his lectures about the deaf. Dr Bell took Helen and Annie to the World Fair in Chicago, a huge exhibition covering 220 hectares. They stayed for three weeks, and one of the most popular 'exhibits' was — Helen Keller. Crowds watched her enjoyment in amazement. She was allowed to touch anything she wanted, go where she liked. She handled priceless diamonds from South Africa, climbed on heavy German guns, fingered rare French bronzes. There was just one thing she refused to touch — an Egyptian mummy!

The quarrel with Mr Anagnos meant that Helen could not return to Perkins. It was a worrying time;

At Niagara Falls

Captain Keller was seriously in debt and could not support Annie and Helen, let alone pay for education. Luckily they had other admirers, who had heard about the pair's courage and achievements and asked to meet them. Some of them were rich and famous, and now they rallied round, offered Helen and Annie a home and paid for private tutoring until Helen could go to a new school. This was the Wright-Humason School in New York which specialised in teaching the deaf to speak.

At Perkins, Helen had been the only deaf child amongst the blind. Now she was the only blind one amongst the deaf, but she amazed the other children by beating them at chess and reading chalk marks on the blackboard with her fingers. She even took part in the school play, moving and speaking her lines when she was patted on the shoulder. Helen and Annie stayed in New York for two years, until Helen was fifteen, and had an exciting time. They went to museums and dog shows, climbed up inside the Statue of Liberty, and met many more famous people. Helen got on well with the deaf children with whom she had 'cosy chats and frolics'. They got up to such mischief as 'playing when we should work, spelling secretly when we should be improving our speech'. But Helen worked hard too, and she left New York determined to go on to university.

This was a staggering ambition and, many people thought, a hopeless one. Women were not encouraged to go on to higher education in those days; it was not fashionable. Helen had elected to go to Radcliffe, the women's part of the famous university for men,

Harvard. First, she had to get into the Cambridge School for Young Ladies, where students were prepared for the entrance examination. The Principal of Cambridge, Mr Gilman, thought it was quite impossible for a deaf-blind student to get into his school, let alone prepare for university. But his doubts turned to admiration when he saw the quality of Helen's work, and realised that, through Annie, she could see and hear and speak as well as anyone.

Helen started by taking courses in German, French, Latin, English, Greek, Roman history and mathematics. A few months later she added physics, astronomy and geometry. It was hard work for Helen, but even worse for poor Annie. There were no special teachers now, and she had to spell all the lectures into Helen's hand. Hardly any of the text books were available in braille or raised print – Annie had to read them all. She had to research everything Helen needed to know, in several languages. Annie had trouble finding a Greek typewriter and a machine for embossing algebra signs. Helen started to fall behind with her work, Annie was blamed and she and Helen got irritable with each other. Then Helen was ill and Annie was blamed for overworking her.

Mr Gilman wrote to Mrs Keller saying that for Helen's sake, she and Annie should be separated. Mrs Keller, not understanding the situation, agreed. Annie may have been outspoken and hot-tempered, and she may have been too ambitious for Helen. She did have her faults – but Helen could not do without her. As their friends said, 'For better or for worse, those two are married for life!' Helen could not believe that anyone would take her Teacher away. But Annie was forced to leave, and nearly threw herself in the river from grief.

Loyal friends rallied again and re-united Annie, Helen and Mrs Keller — but not Mr Gilman. Another school was closed to Helen.

7   The Crusader

Helen got into Radcliffe in 1900 — thanks once more to the generosity of friends and benefactors who paid for her tutors and gave her refuge in a farmhouse for her studies. She was popular at Radcliffe and though she joined in many activities such as swimming and riding a tandem bicycle or a horse, she sometimes felt left out. Passing students may have smiled or said 'Hi' — but they did not reach out a friendly hand to show they were there and Helen missed this. She and Annie had to work much harder than anyone else to keep up so they missed out on the social life. When it came to taking her exams, Helen had no privileges — no Annie at her side. Annie had to leave the building when the papers arrived, and a university official spelled the questions into her hand. She typed them out on her braille typewriter, and answered the questions on an ordinary one. She had taken seventeen and a half courses on subjects, from the English Bible to the history of philosophy, economics to Shakespeare. Her examination papers were so perfectly typed that they were given a place in the university's museum — and she gained her Bachelor of Arts degree with honours.

During her four years at Radcliffe, Helen had been

Helen at Radcliffe College

busy apart from her studies. The short account of her early life that Annie had persuaded her to write for *Youth's Companion* had aroused many people's interest. She was kept busy writing letters, giving her support to charities and helping to launch appeals for the deaf-blind. Above all, she was urged to write a much longer account of her life. For this she needed help from someone who could see, and knew something about publishing. John Macy was the perfect choice. He was a scholar and editor of several magazines; he was also young, amusing and good-looking. He learned the manual language so that he could work with Helen and between 1902-3 they wrote *The Story of My Life* in three parts. First came Helen's own story, then a selection of her letters, and finally an account of her education written by John.

The book was such a success and made so much money that it changed their lives. For the first time they could be independent. Helen and Annie became extravagant, they bought expensive clothes and furniture, travelled in luxury, and after Helen left Radcliffe, bought a 17-room house set in 2½ hectares of land. John Macy was a part of the new household and there were rumours of romance. He adored the young and lovely Helen — but he fell in love with Annie. She was ten years older than himself, but she was amusing, energetic, often saucy, and had always fascinated men. She loved John too, but could not make up her mind about marrying him because of Helen. John insisted that their home would always be Helen's home too, and she finally accepted him when Helen protested that she

John and Annie Macey

could never be happy again if Annie did not marry the man she loved.

In the years between 1905 and 1914, Helen gradually changed from a gentle, rather saintly character into a fighting reformer. Once Annie was happily married, and Helen was freed from endless studying, she began to find out what was really going on in the world. And she did not like what she found. There was social injustice everywhere, and no-one, least of all the government, seemed to care. She cared — and she wrote to friends, politicians, celebrities and newspapers to say so.

Her work for the blind became political. Blindness, she pointed out, was often caused by disease; and disease, as everyone should realise, was caused by living in dirty, overcrowded slums. She had visited slums.

As a suffragette

She wanted to wipe them out. 'How could rich industrialists live in luxury when their workers starved in slums?' she asked. She attacked rich people who gave charity to the poor, but did not ask *why* they were poor, or what could be done about poverty. When the workers started to strike in the mills and factories, Helen encouraged them by sending messages to the 'brave girls'. Many were women whose pitiful wages had been cut and whose children were starving. She believed that women should be allowed to vote for the government that controlled their lives, and became a suffragette. The Suffragette Movement in England supported her and Helen became militant, urging women to demonstrate, go on hunger strikes, break windows until they got their way. She demanded a fair deal for the downtrodden black people, she condemned capital punishment and child labour.

In 1909 Helen and John Macy declared themselves socialists, and Helen, with her growing influence was called 'the toast of socialists, pacifists and feminists.' She was also a great embarrassment to many of her family and friends. By 1914 she had worked so hard on her speech that she could address vast public meetings. She did so as a pacifist, when America was preparing to take part in the war in Europe, urging the workers not to fight for a country that treated them with a clenched fist when they went on strike for higher wages. She was preaching revolution, but being Helen Keller, she got away with it.

8 Helen in Love and in Show Business

John Macy's publishing work and politics kept him away from home more and more. By 1914, Annie, who had become grossly fat and was often ill, realised sadly that her marriage was over. She and Helen had had to take up lecturing to pay for their living expenses, and for John Macy's too, and they were travelling all over the country. Polly Thompson, a young Scotswoman joined the lecture tour as a secretary, hairdresser and bodyguard for Helen. She later became housekeeper as well, and was to stay as a loyal companion for the rest of her life. Polly quickly learned to 'talk' to Helen, who had now mastered lip-reading by putting her fingers on a speaker's lips. Polly became so expert at the manual language that she and Helen would often go to the theatre or cinema together where Polly would spell the plot and dialogue, and a description of the actors' expressions and costumes, into Helen's hand at a speed of sixty-five words a minute.

When the lecture tour ended, Peter Fagan was employed as an extra secretary to help with the huge postbag. He, too, was quick to learn Helen's languages, and one evening, when Annie was very ill, and Helen's mother had come to take her back to Tuscumbia, he asked Helen to marry him. He loved her, and promised to look after her as Annie had always done.

Helen had missed having boyfriends as a student, and she had often thought of getting married and having children. She wanted to marry Peter, but although she was now thirty-six, she did not really control her own life. She was very dependent on other people, and she knew that those who were closest to her would object. They tried to keep their marriage plans a secret, but the cook got wind of them and rushed to tell Mrs Keller and Annie that the couple were going to elope. Annie was too ill to care, but Mrs Keller was furious. She said Peter was wildly political, a bad influence on Helen, and banned him from the house. She was even more furious the next day when she read in her newspaper that Peter and Helen had actually taken out a licence to get married!

Peter and Helen kept in touch with braille notes. He planned to snatch Helen away from her mother when they changed from the boat to the train on the journey to Tuscumbia. But Mrs Keller was suspicious, and took Helen all the way by train. Peter followed them, but he was driven away from the house at gunpoint. The end of the romance is a mystery. All that is known is that Helen packed her bags one night and waited on the porch. But he never came back.

When Annie was better, she, Helen and Polly went back to lecturing — until they suddenly received an offer from Hollywood to make a film about Helen's life. Helen was thrilled. Here was a chance to get her message across to huge audiences all over the world. In

Helen and Polly in Scotland

America alone 15 million people went to the cinema a day! Furthermore, Hollywood was famous then for making people rich — and Helen needed money. She had nothing saved for the future and she wanted security for Annie when she could no longer work.

The film was to be called *Deliverance* and Helen had a rather grand idea of the message she would give mankind. It would be a message of courage, a message of a brighter, happier future for all men. She, who had been in a dungeon of despair, would open the prison doors for all who were bound by circumstances and poverty.

A child actress played Helen as a child, and in the later scenes she played herself. Polly and Annie told her what she had to do in each scene, and the director stamped on the floor when she had to do it. The three ladies had so much fun in Hollywood meeting all the stars that they did not realise what was happening to their film. The producers had decided that it needed livening up, and they added some epic scenes to 'illustrate' Helen's life. One was a complete battle scene in which Knowledge and Ignorance fought for control of Helen's mind in front of the cave of Father Time. The film ended with Helen represented riding a huge white horse, blowing a trumpet and leading thousands of factory workers to 'Deliverance'.

At an early screening, Helen realised that the film was often ridiculous and had strayed far from the truth. But by then it was too late. The film was well reviewed. It did not make Helen rich, but it inspired a musician to dedicate a song, 'Star of Happiness' to her. George

Lewis worked in the variety shows — vaudeville — which were popular in the early 1920s, and he persuaded Helen and Annie to join him. Many people were shocked at the thought of a deaf and blind woman doing an act on a bill with tap dancers, acrobats and performing seals. The rowdy audiences were taken aback too, until Annie and Helen captivated them with their story. Annie opened the act, telling how she had come into Helen's life. Together they acted out the W-A-T-E-R miracle at the well, and then the band played 'Star of Happiness' as Helen was led to the front of the stage to answer questions from the audience.

'Can you tell when the audience applauds?' Annie would ask as the cheers died away.

'Oh yes', Helen replied, 'I hear it with my feet.'

9 'This Beggar's Life'

The American Foundation for the Blind was formed in 1921 with an ambitious and costly programme, which included setting up schools for the deaf and blind, establishing one braille system (there were then several) and embossing more and better books. They could employ expensive professional publicists to raise funds, or, better still, recruit Helen Keller. For Helen, it was an ideal arrangement. She was given work that she loved doing anyway, and a regular income as well.

For three years from 1924, Helen, Annie and Polly travelled America from coast to coast. They spoke to 250,000 people at 249 meetings in 123 cities and raised large amounts of money. Helen called it 'this strenuous beggar's life'. Annie, with her background of poverty, hated begging and always felt the rich looked down on her. She was glad when they took a long break for Helen to write three more books.

But Annie's eyes were painful and her sight was deteriorating: it was difficult to give Helen all the help she needed going through cabinets full of notes, letters and cuttings. Helen's publishers loaned her one of their own staff, Nella Braddy Henney, to help them. Nella found working in the strange household with its fascinating people a rare experience. Helen typed away in the attic and then brought her pages down to be edited by Annie and Nella. Then Nella read them aloud as Annie spelled them back again to Helen. The system worked, but Nella sensed they were not happy delving into the past. They had been through some very painful times. Nella was interested in the way Helen 'saw' things and asked her to describe a city. 'Houses, tramping feet', she said, 'smells from windows, tobacco, pipes, fruit, gas, tiers upon tiers of odours. Automobiles, a whirr that makes me shiver. A rumble.' Nella noted that Helen found New York depressing and tiring. She felt weighed down by the sheer weight of its vibrations.

Nella and Annie chatted as they waited for Helen's work, and Nella realised that Annie's story was as fascinating as Helen's. For the first time since Annie was fourteen, and she was now sixty-one, she talked about her childhood and admitted she had spent six years in the almshouse. Even Helen did not know this.

By 1929 Helen had published three more books and should have been enjoying the success they brought. But Annie had had one of her eyes removed, and the other was painful and had only one-tenth of normal vision. It was Helen's turn to comfort Annie. Helen had been blind since babyhood, so it did not make her sad. But it broke her heart to know her Teacher's sight was fading.

Annie was advised to take a holiday. As luck would have it, the Foundation wanted Helen to go to Europe, and the 'Three Musketeers' jumped at the opportunity.

With President Coolidge

Helen and Annie

They loved England and were thrilled by the old Roman roads, Saxon dykes and Norman castles. But Annie was miserable in Ireland. She hated driving in a grand chauffered car past the fields where her ancestors had toiled and starved. The bogs haunted her. 'The weird rocks watch me', she said. 'I find myself waiting for them to speak to me, and deep down in my soul I know their message will break my heart.'

They travelled to Scotland where Helen collected a degree from Glasgow University, then crossed to France and on to Yugoslavia where they were honoured guests of the Government. The King was charmed by Helen and they had glorious banquets floating down the

Danube in riverboats.

Back at home Annie and Helen were both awarded degrees of Doctor of Humane Letters, and Helen was largely responsible for organising the representatives of thirty-two nations at a World Conference for the Blind, who were all invited to meet President and Mrs Hoover at the White House. But Helen was already working on the next President, Franklin D. Roosevelt. She wrote him sugary letters saying 'Something tells me you are going to be the next President of the Land of the Free and Home of the Brave.' She could be cunning when she was planning to use someone. When Roosevelt was elected she had him in her pocket. 'Anything Helen Keller is for, I am for', he said, and sure enough the blind benefitted from a number of laws during his term in office!

In October 1936 Annie had yet another serious eye operation. Helen and Polly took her to a beach cottage afterwards to recover. To their amazement she staggered down to join them on the beach one day. But she collapsed and they had to drag her back to the cottage sobbing, 'I am trying so hard to live for you.'

She had had a coronary thrombosis, and told Polly that the Angel of Death was coming for her. Polly wrote down her last words. 'Thank God I gave up my life that Helen might live. God help her to live without me when I go.'

10 Helen and Polly

Scarcely a day passes in Helen's diaries when she does not miss and mourn for her Teacher. Polly could not replace her, but she was the next best thing. Annie had secretly watched Polly on the lecture platform, and knew she could present Helen expertly. She had good taste, and would always see that Helen was nicely dressed and well groomed. Above all she was loyal and hard-working. For the next twenty years, Polly kept Helen active and they travelled the world tirelessly for the Foundation. Wherever they went they were treated like royalty, met by huge crowds and showered with flowers and presents.

It was a hard life. People who besieged Helen for autographs and interviews did not appreciate that. When Helen and Polly were not giving lectures and addressing meetings, they were dealing with trunks full of urgent letters. They were often up at 5 a.m. writing and rehearsing Helen's speeches and still working at 10 p.m. By then Polly's fingers were getting wobbly with constant spelling, and Helen's palm felt raw.

Their first trip after Annie's death was to Japan, where they were welcomed in thirty-nine cities as no

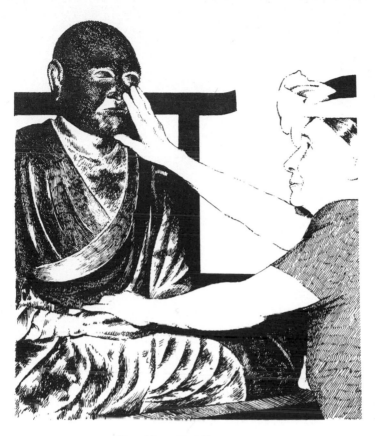

Touching a Buddha statue

king or president had ever been before. Polly reported
that Helen was making history. The Japanese people
believed that the gods gave people their handicaps, so
if they were deaf, blind or crippled, they had to put up
with it patiently. Helen was living proof that handicaps
were there to be conquered, and her influence was so
great that programmes to help the handicapped were
set up and fully backed by the Japanese government.
She was also successful in campaigning for women's
rights — and became the first woman in the world

allowed to touch a sacred bronze Buddha.

Helen took very happy memories of Japan back to America and she was loyal to her new friends even though they were at war with China and becoming increasingly aggressive towards the United States. But then the Japanese bombed Pearl Harbour, drawing America into the Second World War, and Helen was as outraged with them as everyone else. She had been strongly anti-war when the war began in Europe in 1939, but the more she learned about the power-crazed fascists under Mussolini, and the Nazis under Hitler, the more angry she became. She was particularly upset when they forced young children to have a military education. She had always had deep affection for children and was appalled that they should be brought up to violence. She also heard that the Jewish Institute in Vienna had been closed down, and its blind students turned out to beg or starve on the streets. Once Helen accepted that the war had to be fought, she desperately wanted a part in it — her own mission.

There was an obvious role for Helen — visiting wounded soldiers. So many were badly maimed, blinded or deafened — and defeated. Their lives were shattered as hers had been. But she had learned to fight back. She could tell them that. She set off with Polly to visit military hospitals all over America. To many young soldiers she was a legend; they had read about her at school and assumed she had died years ago. But there she was at their bedsides, bringing comfort and hope.

But America had not been ravaged by the war as

Europe had been. Helen received many piteous pleas from European welfare organisations to visit them. She did — and was shocked to experience the aftermath of war, the horror and suffering, the destruction and homelessness. In Japan, she and Polly visited Hiroshima and Nagasaki, where the atomic bombs had been dropped. She felt the faces of people terribly scarred by atomic burns, and vowed to campaign against atomic warfare in any way she could.

The war had created a whole generation of handicapped and destitute people, and put terrible pressure on the existing organisations to help them. Helen could, and did, use her influence on kings, governments and individuals to help. She was not impressed by her visits to the King of Greece or the Pope — they were not doing enough. But she was charmed by Queen Elizabeth (now the Queen Mother). When Helen told her how much she admired her motherly interest in the welfare of the blind and deaf, and the way she had stood beside her people as London was bombed, the Queen replied that she had taken courage from Helen's conquest of her own difficulties.

11 The Last Mile

Helen Keller's driving urge to help the poor, the suffering, and the underdogs of the world was a vital thread in her life. She was a passionate writer and speaker on their behalf — she could also be embarrassing to her friends and relatives, and politically dangerous to herself. Helen knew what she was told, and sometimes, what people chose to tell her, and she did not always see that there were two sides to every argument. In 1917, Annie had told her to hold her tongue about the Russian Revolution. Helen supported the communists, believing that they would give the Russian people freedom, equality and universal brotherhood. She liked the idea of communism without realising that it did not work out like that in reality. She had many communist friends and was lucky to escape the 'witchhunt' in America between 1947 and 1952 when many of them lost their careers and their livelihoods.

  She campaigned for civil rights for black people, rushing through a political minefield where it was best to tread cautiously. The Foundation for the Blind had to hold her back when she travelled for them. It would only harm their cause if she was seen to be dabbling in politics when she visited South Africa with its own black-and-white problem, apartheid; or Israel, where she wanted to reach out a hand of sympathy to the Jewish people, ignoring the fact that the Arabs, rightly or wrongly, had problems too.

Helen was lucky that she never got herself into serious trouble. Being deaf and blind would have been no excuse. But Helen never in her long life lost the power to draw a crowd, or enlist sympathy. She was a survivor. She had always been one.

Arcan Ridge

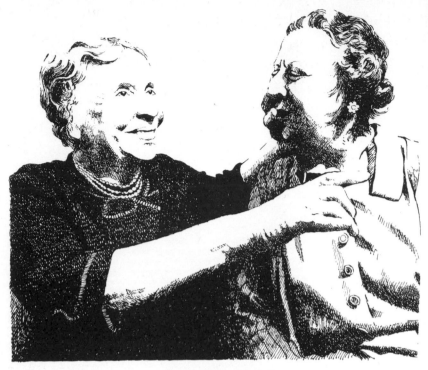

Lip reading with Polly

The Foundation had built a house for Helen and her household called Arcan Ridge. Helen had loved it, especially the gardens, where she had her own roped walk. She weeded, dug in the ground with her hands and even cut the grass. The house was burnt to the ground whilst she and Polly were in Europe. They were touring bombed cities when the news was telephoned to them, and in comparison, one house did not seem very important. There were plenty of willing hands to build it up again.

When they settled down to start writing again in the new Arcan Ridge, Helen was seventy-four. All her papers had been burnt in the fire and she had to start a book she was writing about Annie all over again. She worked at her desk from 7.30 in the morning till 5 in the evening, and she often broke down in tears of anguish as she realised, again, the terrible sacrifice Annie had made for her. Meanwhile a film about her life *The Unconquered* was made and won an Academy Award; and William Gibson wrote a play about her, *The Miracle Worker* which was a huge success on the stage and later as a film. Anne Bancroft, the actress who played Annie on stage, told Nella that she found the audience's reaction strange. The first round of applause was as enthusiastic for her as it was for the actress who played Helen — and then it dried up. Nella said that was exactly how it had been with Annie. Audiences had always trampled on her to get to Helen.

Helen began to show signs of ageing. Her fingers became stiff and less sensitive and sometimes she mixed up the scents of flowers. Polly was not well, and she became so difficult that secretaries and domestic servants refused to stay in the house. She became so jealous of Helen that she would not allow anyone to 'talk' to her, or even let her friends be alone with her. When they called they often found her sitting in a corner, facing the wall and reading.

They were right to worry about Helen being alone with Polly. Polly had a cerebral haemorrage when she and Helen were cooking their lunch one day, but refused to lie down. It was a fearful experience for Helen. As fast as she turned the burners on the stove off, Polly staggered round turning them on again. When she eventually collapsed, there was nothing

Helen could do but wait until the postman came and got help, hours later.

Two efficient and caring women, Mrs Seide and Mrs Corbally moved in to nurse Polly, housekeep and help with the office work. They knew the manual language, but for the next two years whilst Polly was an invalid, they dared not use it in front of her. When Polly died in 1960, they took over and looked after Helen admirably for the next eight years. They bought her clothes, rehearsed her speeches and helped her to stay in public life. Mrs Corbally was a good letter writer and kept in touch with Helen's family and friends. She wrote once that they had 'oodles of fun. Miss Helen was a rogue'. Helen loved hotdogs and they would often slip out to hotdog stands — something that Polly would never have allowed.

At a public function one day Helen said she 'felt funny', but went on to eat a hearty lunch. Mrs Corbally called the doctor, and discovered that Helen had had a stroke. She had to retire from public life at the age of eighty-one. During the next seven years she had further strokes, each one leaving her more confused. It was difficult for her to communicate and she gradually lost control of her life. 'My poor darling' Mrs Corbally wrote, 'is walking that last mile so very slowly.' Helen was slipping back into the isolated world Annie had rescued her from eighty years earlier. But this time it was not a lonely, desolate world. She had lived a full life, and she had been a shining example of hope and courage to a world she never saw and never heard, but always loved.